Martin Glenn
The Best Job in the World

SHOULDERS
OF GIANTS ™

Martin Glenn
The Best Job in the World

Shoulders of Giants™

Compton House Publishing Limited
Compton House
Fairmile Park Road
Cobham Surrey KT11 2PG

www.shoulders-of-giants.co.uk

Compton House Publishing Ltd has
asserted its rights to be identified as
the author of this work.

First published in Great Britain by
Compton House Publishing Ltd.

ISBN 0-9549518-0-8

This book is printed on paper suitable
for recycling and made from fully
managed and sustained forests.

A catalogue record for this book is
available from the British Library.

Typeset in Foundry Sans.

Printed and bound in Great Britain
by Bossprint Ltd, London.

Dedicated to my father, Maurice, who
bought my first packet of Walkers crisps.

Preface

Martin Glenn The Best Job in the World

In recent years, Walkers crisps has achieved iconic status in British life. It is one of the best-loved and most successful brands in the country. Six out of ten households buy Walkers crisps on a regular basis, at a rate of 12 million packs every day.

The man who led the team behind Walkers' success is Martin Glenn. When he joined in 1992, Walkers was a strong regional brand; today it is the number one fast-moving consumer goods brand in Britain, with a 45% share of the £2 billion salty snacks market. Along the way, it managed to double its profitability in just five years.

Martin now heads up Walkers' parent company, PepsiCo, in the UK and Ireland, where he is also responsible for other leading brands such as Pepsi, Quaker Oats and Tropicana, as well as looking after the interests of 5000 staff in ten sites across the region.

In July 2004, Martin was voted the UK's most influential marketer by *Marketing Magazine*. He was *Marketing Week's* Chief Executive of the Year in 2003 and has also been named as a Prince of Wales Ambassador for the East Midlands in recognition of his services in promoting education and volunteering.

In this digital video book, he shares the insights that led to Walkers' success and talks about the skills needed to make sure that a winning brand stays on top. We also hear from the other leading players in the Walkers' story – from the consultants who advised, the agencies who put the campaigns together and even the ex-soccer star who is now as well known for stealing crisps as he was scoring goals for England!

Digital video book contents

Book contents

Acknowledgements

Neil Campbell Vice President Marketing, PepsiCo UK
John Cullip Commercial Director, Walkers 1967–94
Jon Holmes Chairman and CEO, SFX Sports Group (Europe)
Tom Kuzio Snr Vice President Sales, PepsiCo UK
Gary Lineker OBE England Football Captain 1990–92
Vinita Pandey Corporate Affairs Director, PepsiCo UK
Hamish Pringle Director General, Institute of Practitioners in Advertising
Mark Rapley Account Director, DDB London 1978–98
Mark Sherrington Group Marketing Director, SABMiller plc
Founder and CEO, Added Value 1988–2002
Peter Souter Executive Creative Director, Abbot Mead Vickers BBDO
Ellis Watson Marketing Director, News Group Newspapers 1994–2000
John Webster Executive Creative Director, DDB London
Paul Weiland Paul Weiland Film Company

and 5000 members of PepsiCo UK and Ireland – thank you

Foreword

Many years ago, there was a commercial on British TV in which a young schoolboy boasted to his friends that when he grew up he would have the best job in the world. What did he mean? they wondered. Would he be a brain surgeon? The Prime Minister? The Archbishop of Canterbury? No. It turned out that his dream was to be the Chief Taster for Walkers crisps.

In a sense, I grew up to achieve that schoolboy's ambition – even if I do have a slightly different job title – which is why I chose to call this digital video book 'The Best Job in the World'. I'm certainly not suggesting that I and the team at Walkers have done the best job in the world; we've just done the best we could. Along the way we've certainly made mistakes, but as the success of the brand and the business shows, I believe we've learnt from them and got the important things right.

Both in the film and in this book, I try to share some of those lessons. In the film, you hear it from the horse's mouth, and not just from this horse but from many others who have contributed to the success of Walkers. We've had a lot of help from many quarters over the years, both from within the business and from our many external partners. I hope you agree there is something richer and more accessible about seeing and hearing the story told in this way. But it helps to have a written record as well and so there is also this short book to accompany the film.

Martin Glenn The Best Job in the World

I have tried to keep things simple and honest in the same way that as a business we have tried to debate things openly and to apply simple principles. In the book, the important lessons are highlighted as key take-outs. Some of them will perhaps strike you as being plain common sense. But in business, common sense is rarely common practice. At a theoretical level business is really not that hard to understand, but at a practical level there is no doubt it is very hard to do well. After all, there are plenty of business people who will tell you they care about quality, but far fewer businesses who deliver it in a sustained and committed way.

I hope that our commitment to quality is one of the many things that will come out in the book and the film – and, whatever your reasons for reading and viewing, I hope that you find something here to help drive your own business or career forward.

Martin Glenn, March 2005

1. How to Get into a Nation's Lunchbox

Fifty years ago, Walkers was a humble pork butcher's shop in the English Midlands city of Leicester. Today, it's the UK's biggest supermarket brand, with a 45 per cent share of the £2 billion salty snacks market. We reckon that 60 per cent of British households now buy Walkers crisps, at a rate of 12 million packets every day.

Of course, we Brits are famous for our love of the potato crisp (or 'potato chip' to our American cousins). A packet of cheese and onion or salt and vinegar is as much a part of British life as a cup of tea or a plate of fish and chips. Certainly, no British lunchbox, school packed lunch or night in the pub is complete without a pack. But it's also worth noting that making crisps is an industry with almost no barriers to entry. Most British kitchens have the technology to manufacture crisps, so why do more than half of British households choose to buy their crisps from Walkers?

The easy answer to that question is: because Walkers make a damn good crisp. But I also think we've earned our place in Britain's lunchbox by valuing simplicity. We've managed to brand a commodity through the thorough application of imaginative principles. We've been consistent in our aims and values – like our dedication to quality – over a long period of time, and we've been consistently ruthless in the detailed and pragmatic way we've applied them to our business.

Be consistent

> **Consistency** is crucial.
> How **consistent** are your values?
> Are you **consistent** in your strategy?
> Do you have **consistency** in your teams?
> Is your advertising as **consistent** as it could be?
> Is the quality of your products **consistently** flawless?
> Whatever you do in business, it pays to be **consistent**.

But there's also a kind of restlessness at PepsiCo (Walkers' parent company) that means we're never happy unless we're challenging ourselves or trying new things. That can be dangerous in business – meddling with a successful formula is never to be recommended. But I think our trick has been to know when to keep it tight and when we can allow ourselves to let things hang a little looser. Let me give you an example: changing a product specification, like the flavour of cheese and onion, would be a really big deal for us; but we're quite happy to change the name of a product if we think it would get the brand noticed. Many in the UK marketing establishment thought we were reckless when we changed the name of 'Salt and Vinegar' to 'Salt and Lineker', but we just thought – why not? How bad could that be? And in fact it wasn't bad at all. Consumers appreciated it for what it was: a harmless (but attention-grabbing and profitable) bit of fun.

Over recent years, Walkers has enjoyed fairly striking growth by food industry standards, but when you look back over the company's history, it's been a pretty slow burner. Our crisps have long been a source of fierce local pride in Leicestershire, but we took our time to spread ourselves across the country. Even as recently as the mid-eighties you'd have been hard pushed to find a packet in the London area and if you were Scots or Irish you'd have had to wait a good ten years or more to get your hands on a pack in the local corner shop. In fact, when PepsiCo bought the business at the end of the 1980s, the Walkers brand nearly lost out to its arch-rival Smiths, who had been acquired at roughly the same time. Certainly, on paper Smiths appeared stronger in terms of consumer measures such as top-of-mind awareness and saliency. But it couldn't match Walkers for quality, volume or profit, nor could it command the same price in the market – which was probably why we got the nod and went on to become the badge of the megabrand that PepsiCo were looking to create.

The PepsiCo takeover came at the right time for the company. They had fantastic resources as well as a profound understanding of many markets around the world and they were prepared to give Walkers the benefit of both. They also brought us a new sense of professionalism and a fresh burst of energy. But as in any business, luck has had a role to play in the Walkers story, too.

A brief history of Walkers	
1948	Walkers pork butcher's shop introduces a new product: the potato crisp
1966	Distribution expands outside the immediate Leicester area
1970	The Walkers family sells the crisp business to Standard Brands (later Nabisco)
1983	Walkers achieves market leadership in the Midlands and north of England
1986	Disastrous fire at the brand leader Golden Wonder's factory
1988	Walkers is acquired by PepsiCo
1991	Walkers and Smiths (also already owned by PepsiCo) are merged under the Walkers brand
	Tom Kuzio joins as VP of Sales to revitalise the sales system
1992	Martin Glenn, Neil Campbell and Peter Gutierrez are recruited as part of PepsiCo's drive to introduce British management
	The foil pack is introduced
1994	UK launch of Doritos Corn Chips
	Walkers expands into Scotland
1995	Gary Lineker appears in the first No More Mr Nice Guy ads
1996	Expansion into Northern Ireland
1999	Free Books for Schools campaign
2000	Expansion into Eire
2002	Launch of Sensations

When Walkers became the UK's brand leader in the mid-eighties, it was far more by default than design. To be honest, it only happened because one of our main competitor's factories burnt down. Had it not been for that, PepsiCo might well have been looking to invest in Golden Wonder rather than us, when they made that foray into the UK market.

And we also had a stroke of luck with our choice of front man for the long-running Walkers campaign – a certain retired England soccer hero called Gary Lineker ...

In the late eighties and early nineties, Lineker was the golden boy of British sport. He had sprung to international attention in the 1986 World Cup when he had won the Golden Boot award as the tournament's top scorer, despite playing several games with a broken wrist. He went on to captain his country and to score 48 goals for England in 80 games, making him the second most prolific goal scorer in the nation's history. But perhaps even more remarkable was his reputation as a thoroughly nice bloke. Indeed, when he retired from professional sport in the mid-nineties, he'd gone through his entire career without a single booking, let alone a sending off.

Even before he became the public face of Walkers crisps in 1995, Gary had strong Walkers connections. He had grown up in Walkers' home city of Leicester and for a while his uncle, a greengrocer, had supplied the company with potatoes. But in the minds of the British public, Gary also had another association with root vegetables. When the England team were eliminated from the 1992 European Championships after an ignominious defeat by Sweden, *The Sun* newspaper memorably ran the following headline on its back page: 'Swedes 2 Turnips 1'.

One of the main reasons for the defeat, in the minds of pundits and public alike, was the England manager's decision to replace Lineker at a key moment in the match. It's a lesson that Walkers hasn't forgotten: be careful when you substitute Lineker!

Walkers' Lineker campaign has now been running for so long that it's difficult to imagine the brand without him. But it could all have been so different: Gary was very nearly a duck.

In the mid-nineties we were looking for a big idea that could sustain a long-running Walkers campaign and we'd just hired Omnicom agency, BMP. Their creative guys had gone up to the Leicester factory to look for inspiration and had heard lots of people saying to each other in a broad East Midlands accent, 'Ey oop, me duck.' Given BMP's penchant for using animals in their advertising, it was perhaps no great surprise when they said, 'Let's use a cartoon Walkers duck!' What they produced was actually very funny and original, but it wasn't an idea that really captured the brand, the company or our ambition, so we asked them to go away and see what else they could come up with.

On the morning they were due to come in and present their new campaign idea, I briefed my team. 'Whatever you do, ' I told them, 'don't jump to conclusions – don't say yes or no, we must do the overnight test on it.' So the agency walked in and pitched the idea of using Lineker, coming back to Leicester from Japan (where he had just finished his footballing career). He would walk out of the railway station and wander down the street while folk nudged each other and waved at the returning hero. Gary would flash them his dazzling smile, sign autographs and behave as the all-round decent chap that everyone believed him to be. But when he saw a child eating his favourite Walkers crisps, it would all get too much for him. He would ask for the first crisp politely enough, but having tasted it, he'd grab the whole pack and run off munching furiously, with the child in hot pursuit.

When the agency got to the end of the pitch, the brand team, models of professionalism, dutifully told them that comments would be with them in the morning. But I couldn't help myself. 'Bloody fantastic,' I said, 'we'll do it.' Well, everyone slips up sometimes. And you just know it when you see a good 'un.

MEETING STANDARDS
It's about time to:

1 BE PREPARED
- Have clear objectives and an agenda
- Ensure the right people attend
- Do your pre-work

2 SHOW RESPECT
- Start and finish your meeting on time
- Pay attention, avoid talking over others and encourage everyone to contribute
- Stay engaged by avoiding interrupt mobile phones or mess

3 BE ACCOU
- Make it happen an you've commi

PEPSI

2. Laying the Foundations

It would be nice to say that Walkers went from business plan to megabrand in one cunning and brilliantly-executed leap. But of course, it didn't. It was built patiently, from the bottom up, over a generation and more. In recent years, we've refined our brand philosophy into one built around three cores – advertising, sales promotion and in-store merchandising (all of which I'll come to later). But we never forget that those three cores are rooted in solid Leicestershire bedrock: the unimpeachable quality of the Walkers product.

The Quest for Quality

If making quality products were cheap and easy, everybody would do it. But quality costs money and it's tempting for businesses to view it as something they can skimp on or trade off for other product attributes such as image, style or price. But Walkers has never seen quality that way. From the very start, we were prepared to go to unreasonable lengths to achieve consistently excellent quality. The reason for our obsession is simple: crisps taste much better when they're fresh. And, given the number of packets the average Brit consumes in a week, we have to meet the challenge of selling to the world's most discerning connoisseur of the potato crisp. So we must be sure our crisps taste good every bag, every bite.

At the most basic level, quality means ensuring that our raw materials are absolutely top notch. Picking out the spuds with the black bits in might sound easy, but when you're dealing with 350,000 tonnes of them a year, it's a serious business, believe me. Quality also means making sure that our production is second to none. Managing a successful manufacturing business involves mastering every single one of the huge number of repeated actions that go to make up the process. It requires a laser-like attention to apparently mundane detail that British firms are traditionally bad at – which is a shame. Nobody would deny that many British firms are good at flair and creativity. The trouble is that filing a patent is one thing, but turning it into a top-quality, mass-market product is something quite different. And you don't need me to tell you which is more profitable.

Of course, you also need a sense of how the quality of your product compares with other offerings in the marketplace. Most companies test quality against both their own current products and their competitors' products. This can be a useful exercise, but it can also produce an attitude in which a business is satisfied with products that are 'good enough'. The result of this is an inevitable downward drift in quality as products get benchmarked against a declining standard. To avoid this happening, Walkers has developed what we call a 'Gold Standard' crisp – one created from the very best potatoes and fried in the very best conditions. The Gold Standard gives us a True North in quality terms, an ideal of the perfect crisp that we strive to put into every pack, every day of the year – quite a challenge when you depend on a raw material as variable as the potato.

We have also always recognised the role that sales and distribution plays in the quality circle. In the early 1960s a decision was taken to limit the expansion of our distribution to those areas where we knew we could guarantee delivering a fresh product – which, in effect, restricted the company to the Leicestershire area for years. Back then, we would actively discourage the sales force from selling too much product to the same store for fear that they might get sold past their date code, and in certain cases we even stopped supplying outlets altogether if they weren't shifting packs fast enough. Today we don't have quite the same problem, but we still ensure that products are held in the Walkers system for no longer than a few days before getting trucked out to over 2500 delivery locations around the British Isles. In fact, most Walkers crisps are eaten within just two weeks of manufacture.

Developments in packaging technology have helped in our quest for quality, too. For us, packaging is not just about displaying our product to its best advantage, it is also crucial in ensuring that our crisps reach the consumer as fresh as they can possibly be. So we've always seized on any innovation that offered the slightest improvement in packaging, regardless of cost. When we changed from see-though plastic to shiny foil bags in 1992, we were told it would be unpopular because customers wanted to see what they were buying. But we knew that if we put crisps in foil bags, they'd seal better and they'd be less exposed to sunlight, which meant they would deteriorate less quickly. When we started flushing the packs with nitrogen in 1996, some people told us it would be too expensive and therefore unfeasible. But we knew that by reducing the effects of oxygen on our crisps, we could keep them fresher, so we went ahead anyway. In both cases, we decided it was our job to sell people the benefits of the new packaging even if they weren't immediately apparent. As it happened, some consumers noticed the difference right away – and even wrote in asking if we'd changed the product. Of course, we hadn't; they were just experiencing the crisps fresher than ever before.

Ultimately, quality creates a virtuous circle: if you have a high-quality product and you sell it fresh, it will sell faster. Faster sales means higher margins, which give you more money to reinvest in demand-building like advertising and selling, which, in turn, will sell product faster still (see Figure 1). And if you get into that loop, you're in pretty good shape.

Figure 1 The virtues of selling it fresh

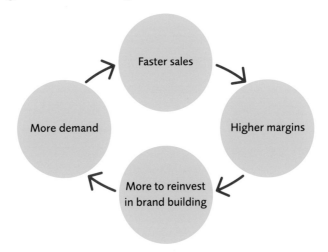

Quality is a journey and never a destination. We believe that you should improve quality as a matter of faith even if you can't prove that people are going to appreciate it. When you eat a packet of Walkers, you can be pretty certain that it's a little bit better than it was yesterday, but not quite as good as it will be tomorrow. As the American novelist Mark Twain once said, 'Continuous improvement is better than delayed perfection.'

Make quality your religion
> Put your faith in quality. Just like Heaven, the rewards are long term and lasting.
> Remember that God is in the detail.
> They also serve who sell and deliver. Praise the role of sales and distribution!

Advertising

When PepsiCo acquired the Walkers business at the end of the 1980s, we had an undeniably great product, but it wasn't yet a great brand. Think of the difference between a good Shakespearean actor and a great Hollywood film star and you'll know what I mean. For both thespians and packaged goods, it's hard to put your finger on what makes the crucial difference between the quality performer and the out-and-out star, but just as for an actor a good first step would be a decent agent, it was imperative for us to get ourselves some truly memorable advertising.

Walkers had been pretty well advertised in the past but it had never been really memorably advertised. In fact, when you look back at the archive you can spot a number of ideas that have cropped up in much more recent campaigns. They had played with the idea of a 'walker' – an absurdly dressed man strutting around the streets giving out packets of crisps to a grateful populace – something which we echoed with our recent walk-o-meter campaign (offering free pedometers to visitors to our website). Interestingly, there was even an appearance by Gary Lineker in his Everton days doing an endorsement to camera. But this time we knew that we weren't looking for a one-off – a simple return for a single spot. We wanted a campaign that would yield compound interest and growth over the long term.

We were convinced that with the right kind of imagination and the more rigorous discipline that PepsiCo brought to the party, we could take Walkers advertising to a completely new level. So we put a lot of effort into understanding the psychology of the brand and what it stood for (see Figure 2) – and we unashamedly used outside help to do so. We asked ourselves questions like:

If Walkers weren't there, how would it be missed?
If Walkers were a person, who would it be?
We used the answers to questions like these to nail a positioning statement which centred on the idea of 'British irresistibility'.

Figure 2 Walkers crisps brand values

Modern classic	Iconic and British	Family friend
Simple pleasure	Fun, Honest, Sociable	Straightforward
Traditional	Shared, Family	Everyday

Source: Walkers Snack Foods Ltd

It was important to understand the values at the heart of the product. Walkers was now a nationwide brand, but it was still true to its roots as a local hero. It's an absolutely top quality product manufactured and marketed with enormous professionalism and attention to detail, but at the end of the day it offers a simple pleasure, accessible to everyone, unpretentious and democratic. We wanted to make it clear to people that although we take our product deadly seriously, we don't necessarily take ourselves seriously. We might look like serious business types, but we also have a strategic belief in the power of humour both as a teacher and as a leveller.

As I described in the first chapter, it took a few false starts before our agency, BMP, came up with Gary Lineker in No More Mr Nice Guy, but when they did, it was clear immediately that it had the makings of a great campaign. It was absolutely bang on brief: Gary really was a Leicester local hero turned national (and indeed international) celebrity, so from that point of view, the fit with the brand could not have been better. The basic idea also had the legs to run and run. The notion that our crisps were so delicious that they could persuade a chap as famously nice as Gary to steal from children was one that could be reworked over and over again in countless different ways.

But good fortune had its part to play. At the time the first ad went to air in 1995, Gary was known as a professional footballer, pure and simple. His career as a TV presenter was still some way off and his acting talents were quite untested (whatever a few defenders may say about the odd tumble in the penalty box). The fact that he proved so telegenic in that very first commercial was a huge bonus; if ever a TV star was born and not manufactured, that was the moment. We were also fortunate that one slack news day, *The Sun* chose to run a front-page story about the campaign. It picked up on a few complaints (somewhere in the region of 12, as I remember) saying that the Lineker ads amounted to an encouragement to children to steal. Well, while we take our responsibilities seriously, especially towards children, it was obvious that this kind of gripe could only come from someone with a major sense of humour bypass, so we decided to score it in the 'any publicity is good publicity' column, take the positives from it and get on with the job. In fact, it had done us a huge favour – it generated an enormous amount of further media coverage and got people talking about the advert right across the country.

On just about every measure, No More Mr Nice Guy was a staggering success (see Figure 3): overall sales growth, market share, value share, ROI, you name it.

Figure 3 Share of crisps market (volume)

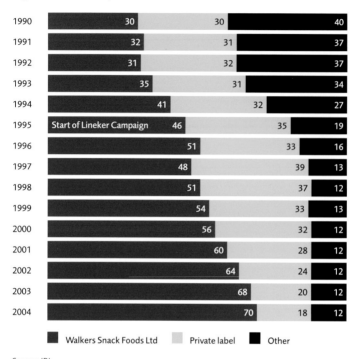

Year	Walkers Snack Foods Ltd	Private label	Other
1990	30	30	40
1991	32	31	37
1992	31	32	37
1993	35	31	34
1994	41	32	27
1995	Start of Lineker Campaign 46	35	19
1996	51	33	16
1997	48	39	13
1998	51	37	12
1999	54	33	13
2000	56	32	12
2001	60	28	12
2002	64	24	12
2003	68	20	12
2004	70	18	12

■ Walkers Snack Foods Ltd   Private label   ■ Other

Source: IRI

So, we said to ourselves, it's hard enough to get noticed in the first place, now how are we going to build on what we've achieved? Our awareness scores for the campaign demonstrated that there was a massive economic case for trying to keep it going. We knew we had enough product news in the hopper to fuel a long-running campaign and we kept seeing adverts written by the agency that could build on that. So we said, let's stick with it and shame on us if we can't keep it fresh.

We knew we could do this for a while simply by putting Gary into different situations – for example, dressing him up as a hippy and getting him to dance down Carnaby Street or gluing a beard on him and putting him in a black and white Ingmar Bergman movie. But the key to keeping it so strong over such a long period has been to play with the storyline conventions. So we've introduced rivals to his 'arch-crisp-thief' role like the young pretender Michael Owen, who gets beaten up by a rugby team for his troubles. We've shown Gary outfoxed by a wilier and more determined enemy such as Steve Redgrave on his turbo-charged rowing machine. And we've also used him in cameo roles in the Sensations campaign, disguised as David Beckham so that he can fool Victoria into handing over her crisps to him.

There's something very British about the quirky humour we use in the Walkers campaign, but the basic concept behind No More Mr Nice Guy seems to have resonance around the world. The idea of a paragon of virtue who is tempted to steal delicious crisps is one that PepsiCo has reworked with local heroes in several other markets: rugby World Cup-winning captain Francois Pienaar is the crisp thief in South Africa, while wholesome singer Marco Borsato is the Dutch protagonist and film star Antonio Banderas does the job in Spain.

Of course, it doesn't take a genius to decide to stick with an obvious winner, but what surprises me is how few companies do it. The problem seems to be that some company cultures accept the idea that the three Rs of brand management are: Repackage, Relaunch, Resign. Certainly, there are brand managers out there who get tired of advertising or pack design or strategy long before their consumers do. And the brand manager who is so anxious to leave a mark that he doesn't have the patience to see through his own operating plan is a dangerous beast indeed.

Staying loyal to Lineker has paid dividends for Walkers. But the campaign hasn't just been consistent in our choice of front man; Walkers has applied the same principles behind the scenes as well. We've still got the same VP of Marketing (Neil Campbell), we've stuck with the same external advisors and we still use the same commercials director (Paul Weiland) as we did right at the start of the campaign. Occasionally, we've needed to refresh the campaign to take it to a new level, which we did by switching agencies from BMP to AMV a few years ago (but we remained loyal to the Omnicom group of agencies and, of course, we kept the same campaign running through the switch). As a result, we've built up a rich fund of instinct, nous, folklore and memory held in the minds of a team of people who have nurtured Walkers' success over a number of years. There must be something in it: more than 50 commercials on from the first Welcome Home ad, the campaign is still going strong.

How to make it memorable

> Know your brand. Understand the values at the heart of your product and be able to express them in plain language.

> Trust your team. Don't hold your creative partners at arm's length; you're all in it together.

> Stick with success. Don't change for change's sake. But hunt down ideas that will inject new thinking and keep things fresh.

Sales Promotion

When I joined Cadbury Schweppes from university in the early 1980s, one of the first concepts I heard about was 'Above and below the line'. The 'line' was an unquestionable fact of marketing life, a bit like the Berlin Wall – something terrifying and impassable that divided two halves of a territory with a rigid and unarguable certainty. But if you stroll though the centre of Berlin today, it's hard to believe that the Wall ever existed, let alone to figure out where it went or why on earth it was there in the first place – and I must say I have exactly the same feeling about the famous marketing 'line'.

I've heard lots of explanations and excuses for it, but at the end of the day, it seems to come down to this: above the line is for the grown-ups and below is for the office juniors. After all, how many head honchos spend the same amount of time with their promotional agency as they do with their advertising agency? There's a certain breed of marketer who is quite happy to talk TV commercials all night, but when it comes to point of sale, then, for some reason or another, they're always far too busy.

But I came to Walkers with a belief that sales promotion worked. I saw it as a great opportunity to innovate, have fun and make a difference – and not just to the top line. I was lucky in that PepsiCo thought along very similar lines. Based on observations of many different marketplaces around the world, they had reached the conclusion that product news drives sales growth. And they were prepared to back it up by taking a very liberal view of the marketing mix. So at Walkers, we banished the idea that a marketing budget should have x per cent spent on advertising, y per cent on sales promotion – and typically zero per cent on selling. Basically, this meant thinking flexibly and working out where we really could generate most bang for our marketing buck. That doesn't mean that we don't attach importance to advertising – of course we do – but we simply realised that it's important not to neglect the many other ways in which people interact with our products. And it's a strategy that has paid off. We don't spend heavily by FMCG standards, so we'd have to say that Walkers marketing has been pretty cost-effective.

We weren't the first people to understand that product news drives sales, but we've been quicker than most at figuring out how to make it work. Too often in marketing, product news is about little more than stamping 'New and improved' on the outside of the packet. Understandably, consumers get sick of it. As people buy our products so frequently, we need to make sure that we engage with them in a more meaningful way. So we try to think of the brand as a favourite character in a soap opera whose story will twist and evolve over a number of episodes. And we do this by ringing the changes at many different levels.

Product news could be something as obvious as the announcement of a flavour upgrade or the launch of a completely new flavour. But it could also be a flavour tailored to a particular season like 'Turkey and Paxo' for Christmas time or even 'limited edition' flavours such as the Great British Takeaway series that we ran in 2003. When our local football club, Leicester City, won promotion to the Premier League we even did a special packet to celebrate the achievement.

We also like to be creative in our promotions. Back in 1993, we innovated by doing 'Instant Wins', which involved putting five-pound notes into certain packets of Walkers crisps. Getting hundreds of thousands of fivers into that many packets was a logistical nightmare, but we succeeded in generating huge word-of-mouth endorsement for the brand and massive sales uplift. It not only created a bit of discussion down the pub but it also gave people an extra reason for putting a bag in their basket when they nipped down to the corner shop – exactly the kinds of thing that a good sales promotion should be looking to achieve.

But the promotion I'm most proud of – and the one that I felt really did make a difference in more ways than one – was Free Books for Schools. We had looked at the success of Tesco's Computers for Schools campaign and asked ourselves if we could implement a similar cause-related marketing programme. Our opportunity came when we heard about a Department of Education initiative to improve the focus on literacy in schools, by introducing a mandatory one hour's reading into the school day. Unfortunately, schools had been suffering from budget cuts over a number of years and so, though they had textbooks, they didn't have enough fiction. To help remedy the problem, we got together with News International, the parent company of *The Times* and *The Sun*, to introduce a joint promotion. The idea was that if you collected 100 wrappers or 100 newspaper mastheads, you would get a free book for your school. Fronted up with a witty TV spot featuring Gary Lineker disguised as a crisp-stealing teacher in a latex mask, the promotion made a remarkable impact. School kids around the country got together to clip coupons, while grown-ups organised community collection schemes – and within four years there were an extra seven million new books in UK schools. I admit that I can't present figures that demonstrate the impact that the promotion had on sales. But what it undeniably did was to drive fondness for the brand. In fact, I believe the campaign did more than anything else to turn Walkers from a great British brand into a loved British brand. And that, as they say, is something that advertising budgets just can't buy.

Just as in the case of advertising, we have built a strong, enduring relationship with a few key suppliers who now really understand the brand. The Marketing Store and an offshoot labelled the 'Big Kick' led by Debbie Simmons, have been responsible for all of our key work.

In-Store Merchandising

You've got to be seen to be sold. The modern supermarket is not so much a shop as a theatre of commerce – one with the longest chorus line you've ever seen. A big store may have as many as 30,000 stock-keeping units screaming for the audience's attention. To sell in this environment you've got to know how to tread its boards: how to grab attention, how to upstage, how to get into the head of the shopper, how to milk the applause. And that doesn't apply just to huge out-of-town-superstores; what works there will transfer quite happily to the local corner shop.

Actually, in-store theatre is something that impulse brands like confectionery, snacks and alcohol have always done well. But when PepsiCo bought the Walkers business, they brought a new level of professionalism to this side of our sales and distribution. In the early nineties, crisps were typically sold out of boxes with holes punched in the top or they were thrown onto shelves in a fairly random way. It was fairly obvious we were missing a trick. Common sense tells you that something with a strong visual appeal will be more tempting than something that looks like it's just been fork-lifted off the pallet in the warehouse. So we worked with the retail trade and proved to them that moving from a cardboard box to a more carefully designed display could improve the rate of sales quite dramatically – we calculated by as much as 22 per cent. This involved an extra labour cost to the store, but as this could be offset by the improved rate of sales, retailers were quite happy to buy into it.

We also play our part by making sure our products look as gorgeous as they taste. This means that our packaging must work as well visually as it does functionally. We pay attention to the way our pack designs look on an individual basis, but we also think through the way the packs work when arranged together on the shelf, to ensure that we can create a visually arresting brand block to attract shoppers from the shopping aisle. Developments in packaging technology have helped us to achieve this. Since the introduction of the foil pack in 1992, the material we use (the 'packaging substrate', in the jargon) has evolved so that the pack now stands much more rigidly on the shelf than it used to, enhancing the point of difference that we are aiming to create.

Bringing goods to life in-store also requires a detailed knowledge of shoppers' habits. We use techniques like video observation to help us understand how people shop, where they purchase our brand and how they feel about that process. To simplify one key trend this research has identified: people rarely make shopping lists these days, but instead wander round a supermarket fairly haphazardly. This means that routes through a supermarket and destination points have become far less predictable, for example, you can no longer rely on the smell of fresh bread from the bakery at the back to 'pull' the customer down the main aisle of a store. As a result, displaying our products in one clearly signed, predictable location is no longer enough – particularly if we are looking to tap the impulse purchase. So we work with our retail partners to stimulate associations by identifying what we call 'points of interruption' and 'points of affinity' in-store. There are lots of ways of doing this. One example is that we try to position our big sharing packs near soft drinks and alcohol, because they are often consumed at the same time and so people make a natural link between them.

The mutual benefits of working with a retail partner to maximise sales in-store are obvious. But the challenge for the brand owner is to see things not just from the shopper's perspective but from the retailer's, as well. That's why I spend a lot of time looking at how our products are merchandised and how they are handled in-store. I believe the world is a dangerous place to view from the vantage point of your desk; you should never confuse sending someone to the front line with going there yourself. So I make the time to go and work in a supermarket for a day or two every year – and I have never regretted a single moment of the experience. Seeing things for yourself can throw up a lot of invaluable insights that might otherwise be missed. For example, we reckon that 26 per cent of out-of-stock situations can be avoided simply by bringing product out of the stockroom and getting it onto the shelf. That means it's our job to ensure that we make the shelf stacker's work as easy as possible, by ensuring that our products can be identified quickly in the stockroom and are simple to move out into the store. It might not sound like glamorous stuff, but we think it's just as important as getting the advertising right.

You've got to be seen to be sold
> Demonstrate to your retail partners the mutual benefits of working together.
> Think through all the ways in which your customers interact visually with your products.
> Do field work. Experience things yourself. Spend time with your retailers and learn everything you can about how your products are handled in-store.

3. Platforms for Growth

Over the past ten years or so, there have been somewhere between 300 and 400 product launches in the UK salty snacks market. And how many of those have really hung on to claim a long-term place in the eating habits of the nation? I would say only three: Pringles, Doritos and Sensations. I can't hide the fact I'm proud that two of them wear the Walkers badge discreetly on the packet. I could be modest and tell you it happened because we just got lucky – and up to a point it would be true, because you don't achieve anything in business unless you get the rub of the green. But brands don't grow by accident. At the most basic level, the only brands that grow are the ones that are looking to grow.

Growth is essential in business. Any business that is not moving forwards is moving backwards; standing still is simply not an option. It's strange, then, that a lot of big multinationals have a reputation for being very conservative. They seem to have a mindset that likes to work within its comfort zone, which tends to make them introspective and reluctant to embrace change. Of course, they can often create the appearance of growth – growth in profits, at least – by cost-cutting. But as a marketer at heart, I believe that the only kind of growth that is really sustainable is top-line growth – growth in revenue and volume. And that is something that can only be achieved by looking outside and focusing on what consumers want and how the resources of the company can best be used to serve them. These days, the only companies that can afford not to have a marketing mindset are monopolies.

Why big brands lose it

There are three main reasons why once-mighty brands are brought low:

1. They lose their quality advantage.
2. They get arrogant about price and think they can command a massive premium versus competitors.
3. They lose contact with teens, who might be quite a small part of the market, but are vital as they represent the next cohort of brand users.

Certainly, at PepsiCo we have always had a relentless growth imperative which encourages or even compels people to do new things. It means that we're a restless bunch. We like to challenge ourselves – and we like to take bold steps. In fact, we believe you won't grow unless you're bold. Life's too short to make small changes to small things all the time. Make small changes to big things or, even better, make big changes to bigger things. That's the way we like it.

And we've found that if you really focus on growth with disciplined management controls, the profits will look after themselves.

Stay restless

> Always have an enemy. It doesn't matter who. Pick on someone or something. Conflict focuses the mind.

> Always create a new goal. Be bold and ambitious in your thinking. Strategy is stretch.

> Always look for new benchmarks. Find out where you under-perform and define your market differently. If you've made it to the top of the tree, it's time to start on the forest.

Of course, we have to be careful where we're bold. But there's a part of our corporate culture that says that in areas where you're not going to break the bank or bet the company, then bolder steps are more effective – and frankly a lot more fun and motivating – than timid ones.

But what counts as a bold step? And how do we make sure we're being bold and not reckless? The best I can do is to look back at a couple of defining moments in Walkers' recent history.

Making the Big Calls

My biggest call was the launch of Doritos in 1994. In the early nineties we were well on the way to establishing Walkers as a megabrand, but we wanted to explore ways in which Walkers' brand properties could be applied across a wider range of products than just crisps. Basically, we wanted to know how far we could stretch it. So we did market research to find out whether we could put the Walkers brand on a piece of confectionery or a cake, for example. Perhaps unsurprisingly, we found that it wouldn't work with anything sweet, but we had a big licence on anything savoury. So we realised there was an opportunity to use Walkers as a quality stamp for other products in a larger portfolio.

Some companies manage their portfolio by treating their products as a stable of competing power brands – Mars, for example, is quite happy to see brands like Mars, Snickers and Bounty go head-to-head in the market. We didn't want to go down this route as it would involve us in the considerable expense of launching new brands as well as undermining the megabrand status that we had built for Walkers. Of course, we could have decided to launch a series of Walkers brand extensions, but we felt that this ran the risk of spreading the name too thinly and losing impact. So we settled on a 'sun and planets' model in which Walkers crisps was the 'sun' brand providing a centre of gravity and a quality halo for a number of other snack brands, which would gain lustre by their association with Walkers but still retain their own identities. The big question was: which product or products, exactly?

If you compared the US and UK markets at the time, the most noticeable difference was in the tortilla chip market. In the US it was massive, while in the UK it was pretty small and dominated by a small aspiring brand called Phileas Fogg. They had a fairly upmarket positioning, which relied on hot flavours and had a harder texture than the Doritos chip that PepsiCo produced in the States. We believed there had to be potential for Doritos to move into the UK market, but could Brits be persuaded to purchase corn chips in significantly higher volumes? And how would they react to this then unheard-of American brand? When we concept-tested Doritos corn chips versus Walkers-Doritos corn chips, we discovered that the Walkers quality stamp gave us a 12-point difference. We concluded that this added familiarity should allow us to mainstream corn chips into the UK market for the very first time – and to take advantage of this potentially huge opportunity.

But although the market research looked safe, the investment decision was far from it. To launch Doritos would require putting a new team and a new factory in place at a cost of a not insignificant £15–£20 million. And all on the basis of a hunch that people would change a lifetime's buying habits and start consuming a completely new product. This was sweaty palms time. Close cousins we might be, but there is still a long and ignominious history of products and cultural habits that didn't quite transfer across the Atlantic. Drive-in movies, anyone? Baseball? Pumpkin pie? Double-dating? The Superbowl? Aren't we the classic case of two nations divided by a common language? PepsiCo had also had a tough time with two previous UK launches of Stateside successes – a corn curl called Cheetos and a ridged crisp called Ruffles, both of which had lacked the significant points of difference to make the desired impact on the UK market. I was pretty certain that Doritos was another case altogether, but there was certainly enough material there to build a fairly convincing nightmare scenario.

Thankfully, I'm not a pure gut-feel decision-maker. Over the years we've developed a range of product tests that help us work out whether a product has got a chance of beating the odds in the marketplace. And that's reassuring, to say the least. I also invest time in sifting out what appear to be unconnected facts and then making rules from them. But I can't deny that I use my intuition to narrow down options. I use data but I have a healthy suspicion about how much data can inform a decision. I reckon I'm paid to take a decision on the basis of 80 per cent of what I need to know and then a judgement on top of that. At the end of the day you just have to go for it: you have to accept that all decisions have an element of courage in them.

Of course, it helps that I have such a trusted team around me in the company and such a respected group of external advisors to turn to when we need a different perspective. But at a certain point in any debate someone needs to hold their hand up and take responsibility for the decision. It can be a tricky moment, particularly if it comes at the end of a lengthy and passionate discussion and you know that others in the room are not convinced by the arguments. In that situation I use what I call a 'Gimme'. The people I work with know that I won't allow myself more than two or three 'Gimmes' over any major issue, but they accept that at a certain point I may have to look someone in the eye and say, 'This is one of my "Gimmes"; you'll just have to go with me on this.'

Once we had the business case for Doritos together, we wanted to get into the market fast. And assembling a cross-functional team that could get a new factory up and running and train our new recruits was vital. Our people knew that if they could make Doritos successful it would be a step change for the business. So to pull it off would be seen as something remarkable (in the packaged goods world at least) – both a source of pride and a great business memory. And we did it. We got a new factory up in record time and, within three months of launch, we had tripled the size of the tortilla chip market in the UK.

There were certainly some wrong turns along the way. Frankly, it would have been surprising if there hadn't been. Despite our best efforts, we didn't manage to nail a positioning for Doritos as successfully as we had done for Walkers, which meant that we didn't find a really successful advertising campaign until we came up with 'Friendships' about four or five years down the road. We were also probably too conservative with our pack formats. Because we wanted to mainstream Doritos, we focused on small packs and multi-packs to suggest that people could eat them in the same way as crisps. This meant that we were a bit slow in introducing big bags. And when our marketing VP Neil Campbell took the plunge and decided to do so, it added a significant layer of growth for the business and allowed us to build a dip business on the back of it, too. With the benefit of hindsight, you'd have to say that was something we should have done earlier.

But in any new project you need to build in the idea of a batting average. In cricket, each time you walk out to bat you know full well that you could be walking straight back in again one ball later with nought against your name. It has happened to the greatest names in the sport, sometimes twice in the same match. But over a season, or several seasons, or a career, these things should even themselves out. If you can offset a couple of disasters with a couple of spectacular successes and leaven the whole enterprise with a few solid performances, you should end up with a pretty reasonable batting average. And that was the case with Doritos. We had the talent, we had the technique, we had the guts to lead the market and there was nothing wrong with our fundamental proposition.

Decision-making

> Before you make a call, research the hell out of the issue. But accept that all decisions have an element of courage in them.

> Allow yourself two or three 'Gimmes' on any big issue – times when other people just have to accept that you're the one who'll carry the can.

> When you're assessing the success of a project, build in the idea of a batting average; you won't get everything right first time.

Innovating for Growth

I consider Doritos my biggest call because the stakes were so high. And that's not just the size of the financial investment; when I talked to the new recruits at the factory in Coventry on the day it opened, it brought home to me just how much further my responsibility went. But although the stakes were high, I knew the odds were in our favour. Doritos had been a success on one side of the pond so, despite all the dark nights of paranoia, there was no reason why we couldn't adapt and apply the lessons we had learnt to make it work over here. Sensations, on the other hand, was a different matter entirely.

With Sensations, the stakes were not so high, but the odds were certainly far less favourable. All business ideas start with an insight – or, better still, a whole clutch of them – and, for us, the Sensations project kicked off because our research was telling us that people weren't eating Walkers crisps in the evenings – well, certainly not as much as we'd like them to, anyway. Part of the reason for this was that we were just too successful at getting into the nation's lunchbox, so people were looking for something slightly different when they got home after work. But as evenings represented the single biggest snacking occasion (accounting for 24 per cent of snack consumption – see Figure 4), this was certainly not something we could leave unaddressed.

Figure 4 Distribution of snacking occasions: Walkers vs All snacks

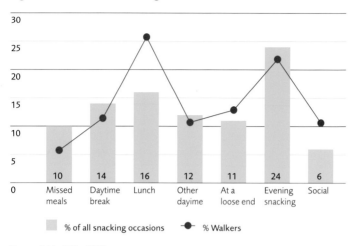

Source: Added Value 1999

When we looked into it a little bit more, we discovered that evening snacking was dominated by indulgent foods such as ice cream, chocolate, cakes and sweets, which were looked on as a treat at the end of the working day – something to help people unwind and relax as they put their feet up in front of the TV. In salty snacks, Pringles massively over-indexed compared to Walkers in the evenings because it offered just the kind of indulgent treat cues that people were looking for. The final piece of the jigsaw fell into place for us when we realised exactly who these people were. Our research showed that women, especially those with children, were very important to evening snacking as they saw this as a time when they could relax and indulge their own needs rather than those of their employers or families. The opportunity was captured very neatly in a Five Ws analysis (Who eats What, When, Where and Why):

Who? Women, especially those with children
What? Indulgent treats
When? In the evening
Where? At home
Why? To unwind and relax at the end of the day

Armed with these insights, the team, led by Neil Campbell and Jon Goldstone, started to develop a proposition for a new product that would be aspirational enough to appeal to the evening snacking consumer, but accessible enough to sit comfortably in the Walkers stable. We saw the opportunity as 'Premium Mainstream' and defined the brand platform with the simple, but memorable line:

Posh crisps from Walkers

The word 'posh' was absolutely crucial because, as a slang term for smart, elegant and exclusive, it summed up the almost contradictory 'down-to-earth, up-market' positioning we were looking for.

In developing the product itself, our R & D people had two variables to play with: the base and the flavour. We had learnt that consumers expected a 'Premium Mainstream' crisp to have a crispier, crunchier, slightly thicker feel than an 'everyday' crisp, while the flavours needed to be a little more 'grown up' and 'authentic'. We figured that a typical everyday flavour such as 'Cheese and onion' would translate into 'Parmesan and caramelised red onion' as a premium flavour, which gave us the chance to split the difference and create 'Four cheese and red onion' to meet the needs of the 'Premium Mainstream' segment in between.

I'm probably making it sound as if the whole project was driven by research – and up to a point it was – but there was still room for a bit of intuitive-thinking. Pre-launch we found that the Thai Sweet Chilli flavour always tested badly, I suppose because it seemed a bit challenging. But we all really liked it – and it was certainly the pack in the office that was secretly eaten the most – so we decided to trust our instinct and launch it anyway. And you know what? It has now become our best-selling flavour with the highest repeat purchase. Which just goes to show that there can be a big difference between what people really like and what they say they want. So when you use market research, don't be like the drunk found leaning on the lamppost – remember it's not there for support, it's there for illumination.

Finding a name for the new product that offered the appropriate adult indulgence cues was a real headache. We tested some like 'Couch Potatoes' and 'Sundowners' which almost made it, before we settled on 'Sensations' as a name which conjured up the taste sensation at the same time as referring in a light-hearted way to the pleasure of eating them. It also passed the 'shopping list test' of being a name that people could remember and write down easily. We backed up the message by using a pack that communicated adult food values and sent out clear signals that this was a serious competitor in the Premium market. We felt that the use of white on the packet was a particularly bold step, as it's a colour normally associated with private label or generic products.

The advertising for the launch centred on the use of Victoria Beckham, aka 'Posh' Spice. Even if she hadn't been known as 'Posh' she would have been a perfect fit for the brand: her public image already embodied the Mainstream Premium position we were seeking and her marriage to one of Gary Lineker's successors as England captain provided a neat link to the parent brand. In fact, you might think she was a blindingly obvious choice as brand ambassador, but things only seem that way with hindsight, believe me. The main focus of the ads was to send up Posh's 'poshness' by showing her doing things like wearing a crown, sitting on a throne and ordering her servants about. This allowed us to reinforce the message that Sensations was an indulgent treat, while suggesting that it was sufficiently down-to-earth to be enjoyed on a regular basis. Gary Lineker was used in a small cameo role to make the connection with Walkers but we were careful to make sure he didn't swamp the execution.

The use of Posh generated a real multiplier effect for us. There was huge media excitement with numerous photographs, articles and features in the tabloid press and gossip magazines. We estimated the free column inches were worth in the region of £2 million of equivalent media spend. She also brought tremendous talk value to the new brand, creating a buzz in workplaces, shops and pubs, as people discussed, gossiped and joked about her appearance in the ads. (More recently we've had a similar success with Posh's successor, It-girl Tara Palmer-Tomkinson.)

As with everything we do, we backed up the advertising campaign with sales promotion and extensive in-store merchandising. In fact, so successful were our point-of-sale materials that we managed to gain around six miles of fixture space in grocery and eight miles in impulse in shops and supermarkets across the country.

The launch was such a hit that it took us by surprise, with sales exceeding target by 200 per cent inside the first year – in fact, in the early days we even experienced capacity problems at our factory as we struggled to keep up with demand. After only twelve weeks, Walkers Sensations had established itself as the third biggest brand in the market behind Walkers standard crisps and Pringles, with a share of nearly four per cent.

I claimed that Sensations is an example of innovating for growth. But when you look back over the story, you'll find no 'eureka' moment of inspiration or breathtaking stroke of genius. There are no crazed scientists making momentous discoveries or wild-eyed blue sky thinkers. So where, you might ask, is the innovation in the tale? For me, the fact that the story of Sensations lacks all the clichés that we have come to associate with creativity is really the key point. Innovation in business rarely if ever proceeds in giant leaps; it is far more likely to edge forward in lots of small incremental steps. Improving a product that people already like and are happy to pay for is often better than re-conceptualising people's habits entirely. After all, a great many innovations have been brought to market over recent years, but how many have stuck? What was the last new product that really made a difference to the way that people live their lives? I reckon you'd have to go back twenty years or so to the first mass marketing of the personal computer.

Having great ideas is one thing, but turning those ideas into vehicles for growth is something quite different. The ideas that succeed in the market are not necessarily the most brilliant ones, but the ones that are driven by companies that know how to put a total business strategy behind them and how to follow it through with a ruthless attention to detail.

Innovation
> All business ideas start with an insight – or even a whole clutch of them.
> Market research can be a lamppost to show you the way, but it should never be something to lean against.
> Don't expect to innovate in giant leaps. Most innovation proceeds by way of small but accumulative incremental steps.

4. Galvanising the System

The journey of a crisp from the potato field to the taste buds is bewilderingly complex. It involves millions of small steps and tiny transactions, not to mention thousands and thousands of people: farmers, factory workers, truck drivers, salespeople, shopkeepers ... the list goes on. These are the ones who make the strategy happen. But the fact is that no one person and no one part of the system holds the key to the whole. A business system this complex relies on delegation, devolution, empowerment and motivation. In short, you have to trust people – people who are prepared to go the extra mile make a massive difference to any organisation.

In a multi-touch-point business like ours, however, where individual actions can have a huge multiplier effect, these people are absolutely crucial. When you make 12 million packets of anything a day, a person who can make a one per cent difference anywhere in the chain can save you an awful lot of money. So when we say we treat every single one of our employees and partners with consideration and respect, we mean it. After all, we're not doing it just because we're nice people (although we'd like to think we are); we're doing it because there's a cast-iron business case for it.

It's easy to be cynical about this kind of thing. Most of the big beasts in the corporate jungle seem happy to trot out a few glib phrases about how they value their staff and put people first – even the ones who are famous for treating their workforce as dog food. So how do we make sure our lofty sentiments are not just so much hot air?

Building Employee Regard

We believe what gets measured gets done, so around the world PepsiCo has a formal process of checking what we call 'employee regard'. Basically, this means finding out what people think and how they feel about working for us. And though we regularly get results showing that 85 per cent of employees are proud to work for us, it gives us no grounds for complacency. We make sure we act to remedy any grievances and use the findings as a basis for continually improving the relationship between employer and employee.

We also believe that people who work for us should have a stake in the business, so each year everybody gets ten per cent of their wages in PepsiCo stock. It makes perfect sense to do this, as the more closely we align the company's interests with those of the workforce, the more motivated our people should be. But it will only work if they understand what the company is trying to achieve and what their shares really mean; after all, there is no reason why a front-line packaging film operator should take an interest in the arcane workings of the stock market.

So we have a formal programme of business education for every employee. We try to explain how a commercial organisation works, how we find out what consumers want and how we make the products that meet those needs. We also discuss fundamental issues such as why it's necessary to make a profit and what level of profitability is right for our business. This might sound like obvious stuff, but until recently there were very mixed attitudes to the idea of profit – certainly in the UK. In the USA and to some extent in continental Europe too, the market has been accepted as the pre-eminent mechanism for the running of the economy for at least 50 years. But until perhaps as late as 1997, with the election of an avowedly market-friendly 'New Labour', there was still a very polarised view of profit in British society – and for many people 'profit' was still a dirty word. So we felt it was important to give people our take on the issue, although we're careful to make sure this is not a propaganda exercise, so it's not just about spreading the good news; it's also about keeping a sense of balance. Business is a tough old game and there will occasionally be blood on the mat; but most people understand that. And the thing I really enjoy about it is that we now have hundreds of people on the shop floor who will chat to me quite freely about our share price, our growth forecasts or even the current p/e ratio – and I gamely try to bluff my way through it all!

Martin Glenn The Best Job in the World

The return on investment from these kinds of programme is crystal clear. We are blessed with very good people; both our staff turnover rates and our accident rates are far lower than average. And those two facts are closely related – experienced people in a factory understand what's going on around them and are more likely to have ongoing dialogues with supervisors and managers. That means that faults are picked up early and action can be taken before anything goes seriously wrong. It also means that we get considerable input from shop-floor employees into all aspects of the business from improving productivity to the kind of flavours that are trendy with their kids at the moment.

Respect

> Anyone in an organisation who is prepared to go the extra mile is worth their weight in gold. Nurture those people.

> Make sure that everyone in the company understands how the business works and make them proud of what it's trying to achieve.

> Minimise your staff turnover. Employee loyalty pays dividends in all kinds of ways.

The High-Performance Team

Since Frederick Taylor introduced the time and motion study back in the late nineteenth century, manufacturing industry has been associated with the 'command and control' management model. The system is based on a fairly crude analogy with the human form, in which management is the brain and the workers are the body. So orders are formulated at the top and then communicated down through a rigid military-style hierarchy to the limbs and digits which actually do the real work. It's a great system if you happen to be an army general. The trouble with it is, it doesn't work. It probably never did work as effectively as people claimed, but in modern business, it just doesn't work at all. Things move too quickly these days for people to be able to waste time on the games of Chinese whispers that middle management used to play as they passed information up and down the chain of command. Resources are too valuable to be squandered on the extravagant displays of privilege and deference that senior staff used to treat as their birthright.

The favoured analogy in business today is that of the team – a football team, a company of actors, a unit of special forces, take your pick. Although if you want to position yourself at the leading edge of business fashion, you'll know that any old team just won't do; what you're really looking for is a high-performance team. Not that there is anything very new about a high-performance team – in fact, the only way it differs from any other kind of team is in the quality and quantity of its output. But people have started getting interested in high-performance teams simply because they seem to happen so rarely.

It's always difficult to get a team to gel and too often their output seems to amount to far less than the sum of their parts. So how do you improve the odds on creating a high-performance team?

The principal rule is: don't have a committee of the great and the good. Assemble a group of people who really know their stuff, regardless of their job titles or where they happen to sit in the company hierarchy. And don't compromise on this: it's better to have an empty seat at the table than a timewaster in your midst. But you also need to think beyond the strictly functional roles of your team members. You have to find people who are smart enough to understand what their mission is and diverse enough to spark off each other. You also normally need one contrarian in there who doesn't mind getting under other people's skins.

How do you find these kinds of people? It's important to think through the different personalities as well as the different skill sets that people bring. Of course, you need intelligent people (although intelligence can be an overrated attribute in business), but you also need people with drive, who are results-oriented, open-minded and eager to learn. I've always thought that a scintilla of doubt is a good thing to have in a character, because it tells you that a person wants to go on learning. Profiling people psychographically (which is cheap, quick and effective) can also help to ensure you get the right blend of personalities by reducing the guesswork involved.

Managing team meetings

> Ask to learn. Questions are one of a manager's most useful tools. But don't ask questions to prove a point. And don't use them to catch people out. Let them help you focus on the problem and bring in other views.

> Discuss your mistakes. If you are open and honest with other people, they will be more inclined to return the favour.

> Don't punish failure. Brainstorm, don't blamestorm.

Martin Glenn The Best Job in the World

The way the team is handled is also crucial. I've never seen a high-performance team that was micro-managed – you need to recognise people's abilities and give them enough room to express themselves and make mistakes. And this applies to the way that budgets are set, just as much as it does to the way that you deal with the personalities involved. Set budgets too tight and you can be sure that no one's stealing from you, but they'll also be scared to death of taking any risks. So, create a climate where people are not punished for mistakes and give them some wriggle-room, so that they can cover themselves if things go wrong.

It's also good to set objectives that stretch people. I've noticed that if people are optimistic about what they can do, they will achieve more than if they're pessimistic. For 'optimism' here, I read 'stretch'. So, when setting objectives, talk to people about what might be possible rather than what is impossible. Of course, you want people to be analytical and to be realistic in their response to data that they're presented with, but they should also feel able to stretch beyond their immediate conclusions and reach out for more ambitious and imaginative scenarios. You can help people do this by making sure that reward and recognition are clearly visible and by letting them know that you see their work as being about more than just profit or market share. Get them to understand how their work fits in with the broader societal aims and values of the business.

Three rules for high-performance teams

1	Don't have a committee of the great and the good. Get together a team of people who really know their stuff.
2	Don't micro-manage. Give people the space and financial freedom to express themselves.
3	Set objectives which stretch people and help them to see how their work fits in with the broader societal aims of the business.

Working with Suppliers and Trade Partners

Galvanising the system is not just about the people who work for us, it's also about the people who work with us – our many suppliers and trade partners. A lot of companies take an adversarial position in these relationships. They see them as little more than a long-running haggle on quality, price, terms, conditions, delivery times. That doesn't sound like a lot of fun to me; we'd prefer to think of ourselves as the classic 'tough but fair' kind of business. Though, having said that, I'm probably not the best person to judge – I have a suspicion that people only tell you if you're a soft touch or an utter bastard several years after you've retired.

A way to short circuit that problem is to look at things from a technical rather than an emotional standpoint. So we take a long-term view with our suppliers, because we've worked out that it's to our advantage to do so. In purchasing potatoes, for example, we work with long-term contracts, whereas most of our competitors buy in the spot market. To put it simply, we fix the price we purchase at for some time in advance, while our competitors let the market set the price for them and buy from whoever offers the best deal at the time. The downside for us is that when there are good potato harvests and the price falls, we can't take advantage of it; although, of course, when the harvest is poor and the price rises, it works in our favour. More importantly, this arrangement gives our suppliers a predictable future income which offers them security and allows them to plan. And we think it's worth it, as we find the loyalty shown on both sides produces benefits in terms of both quality and productivity.

We apply the same pragmatic principles to our relationship with the trade. For a lot of manufacturers, this relationship is dominated by the issue of price. That's what buyers always want to talk about. But we don't want to discuss price with them; it's a waste of our time. We'd much rather work on ways to develop the market. So we have a completely open and defendable price list. All our customers can see that there are no special deals. The price they buy at is a function of how big they are, how much they buy and how fast they're growing. It means that Walkers is never embarrassed by a price, even when a buyer moves from one chain to another or when a new supermarket chain is set up. And it frees up our time to work on ways of achieving growth, which is something that benefits all the parties concerned.

There is always a degree of healthy tension in relationships with suppliers and trade partners. Everyone is interested in getting the best price for themselves, but bullying relationships achieve little in the long term. Hard-nosed business sense tells us that if you treat people decently, you get far more out of them. And an enlightened attitude towards people is just one way in which we address the broader responsibilities that corporations are now acknowledging: our place in the world.

Don't treat them like outsiders

> Take a long-term view of all these relationships.
> Think carefully before you buy from the cheapest supplier. Staying loyal to your suppliers can pay off in terms of quality and productivity.
> Recognise that price is important to your trade partners, but get them to see that growth is far more important to all concerned.

5. A Place in the World

What is our contribution to society? We make nice crisps and we hope people enjoy them. It doesn't sound much, does it? It's not a cure for cancer or a prescription for world peace. We know that. That's why we say we take our product seriously, deadly seriously, in fact, but not ourselves. Our job is to sell people things they like. Why shouldn't we walk into work with a smile on our faces?

But that's not quite the whole story. Over recent years, most major corporations have started taking their reputation and responsibilities more seriously than ever before. Those that are not doing so will soon be compelled to, as governments tighten legislation to ensure that scandals like Enron are not repeated. But corporate reputation should be about far more than reining in corporate crime and maintaining minimum standards. We believe that our licence to operate is given to us by wider society, which will judge us on the role that our company and our brands play. That probably sounds sanctimonious, but it's not: look at the bottom line and you'll find it also makes perfect business sense.

The Health Challenge

When I started out in business, I knew several people who made a moral decision not to work in tobacco or alcohol, but when I joined Walkers I never expected to walk into a politicised food environment. To find PepsiCo, Walkers and the food industry in the middle of a debate about obesity could perhaps have been predicted, but when the media started pointing the finger and accusing us of contributing to a decline in the well-being of the nation, I still felt a strong sense of indignation.

How do you deal with this kind of negative press comment? Stick two fingers up? Attempt a dialogue? Give up and get a new job? Well, first of all, you need to realise there are too many newshounds hunting too few stories, and issues can get out of proportion. So you have to develop a fairly thick skin and understand that the bigger you become, the more of a target you are. But you mustn't have too thick a skin.

Four or five years ago a company like ours might have said, 'We just make the stuff; it's up to you how much you eat.' And I do genuinely believe that we are not uniquely the problem – after all, crisps only account for a tiny percentage of calorific intake; the problem is clearly one of modern lifestyles. But we have to be sensitive to the way the obesity debate is developing. We want to be part of a society-wide discussion and we have to think through how our consumers feel about the issues involved.

If people's attitudes towards food are changing, it's our job to make sure we adapt so that our brands stay relevant to the way they want to live their lives. Enduring brands provide solutions for people, but as circumstances change the problems they solve have to be re-defined. Packaged food has always been useful to people leading a busy life, but now consumers are also seeking to optimise the balance between calories and nutrition, and we have to respond to that. That's what we've always done in the past and it's why Walkers has lasted as long as it has. To put it simply: if we want to stay in business for another 50 years, we need to make sure we're part of the solution and not part of the problem. Our customers have to feel that we and our brands are still helpful to them.

So we've got a whole raft of initiatives that will make tackling obesity and achieving a balanced lifestyle easier for people. We're reformulating our products in a number of ways, for example by reducing the saturated fat content of our crisps, and we're offering new products that will give people greater choice in what they eat. We're also doing our best to raise awareness of health issues, with initiatives like our free walk-o-meters, which enable people to see just how much they walk in a day. Research shows that most diets don't work in the long term. The most effective way to prevent weight gain is to make small incremental changes in lifestyle, for example, by reducing the amount of calories you take in and increasing the amount you expend. We believe that our initiatives will help people to achieve this by working with the grain of their lives, instead of attempting to revolutionise them as so many quick-fix solutions claim to do.

Of course, there are good business reasons for these kinds of initiative. You might like to call it enlightened self interest. But we also do it because we're citizens, parents and human beings, too.

Corporate Responsibility

Consumers are far more sceptical about business than they have been for a long time. They are also better informed about business than ever before and far more interested in knowing what the company behind a brand is like. So it's crucial that we operate in a transparent way and that there is consistency between the brand and the parent company. Brand management is no longer just about the new ad campaign or the latest sales promotion; it's a discipline which requires 360-degree vision. It's about ensuring that all the constituent parts of a company and its method of operation dovetail at every touch-point with the brand proposition.

This suits us, because we believe corporate responsibility starts at home. We have to be a good employer, because we can't have 5000 people bad-mouthing us to their friends while we're trying to present a decent image to the world. We also understand the contribution that safe, dependable, well-paid jobs make to the community. So we're one of the few companies to have kept a final salary pension scheme at a time when many others are abandoning theirs. And as I mentioned earlier, every employee receives part of their salary in stock so that all of them have a stake in the business.

It's also about being a good neighbour – about controlling emissions from our factories and optimising the way we use our resources. But it goes beyond that. We like to think we can reach out into society and play a useful and responsible role. Our Free Books for Schools promotion, for example, allowed us to develop a Reading Buddy scheme in which we gave staff time off work to go into schools and help kids with their reading. The result wasn't just an improvement in the reading age of children – we also found we had far more motivated employees.

You could probably make a good business case for any of our social responsibility programmes but, to be honest, that would be to post-rationalise. You really have to ask yourself why you do these things in the first place. And it's not because it's the quickest way to the quickest buck or because it gets you a few free column inches in the local newspaper, because that doesn't really come into it. Nor is it a simple salve for the conscience. You do it because it's a statement of the kind of business you'd prefer to be. For sure, you need a business case for this kind of thing, because if you do something solely on moral grounds it won't stand the test of the first profit warning. But in my experience, the initial business case is rarely compelling enough to get you to start the initiative in the first place. It's something you just have to want to do.

I'm not pretending we're holier than thou on this. But I am completely confident that if we opened up our doors and showed people how we operate, they would be impressed enough to say, 'Yes, that's what I would expect from the company behind the Walkers brand.' And that's good enough for me.